Against The Epistle of Manichaeus, Called Fundamental

Against The Epistle of Manichaeus, Called Fundamental

St. Augustine

Against The Epistle of Manichaeus, Called Fundamental

© Lighthouse Publishing 2018

Written by: St. Augustine (Nov.13 354 – Aug.28 430)

Translated by: Rev. Richard Stothert, M.A.

Updated into Modern U.S English by A.M. Overett (b. 1960)

All rights reserved. Without limiting the rights under copyright reserved above, no part of this publication may be reproduced, stored in a retrieval system, or transmitted, in any form or by any means (electronic, mechanical, photocopying, recording or otherwise), without the prior written permission of the copyright owner of this book.

Published by
Lighthouse Christian Publishing
SAN 257-4330
5531 Dufferin Drive
Savage, Minnesota, 55378
United States of America

www.lighthousechristianpublishing.com

Chapter 1. —To Heal Heretics is Better Than to Destroy Them.

1. My prayer to the one true, almighty God, of whom, and through whom, and in whom are all things, has been, and is now, that in opposing and refuting the heresy of you Manichæans, as you may after all be heretics more from thoughtlessness than from malice, He would give me a mind calm and composed, and aiming at your recovery rather than at your discomfiture. For while the Lord, by His servants, overthrows the kingdoms of error, His will concerning erring men, as far as they are men, is that they should be amended rather than destroyed. And in every case where, previous to the final judgment, God inflicts punishment, whether through the wicked or the righteous, whether through the unintelligent or through the intelligent, whether in secret or openly, we must believe that the designed effect is the healing of men, and not their ruin; while there is a preparation for the final doom in the case of those who reject the means of recovery. Thus, as the universe contains some things which serve for bodily punishment, as fire, poison, disease, and the rest, and other things, in which the mind is punished, not by bodily distress, but by the entanglements of its own passions, such as loss, exile, bereavement, reproach, and the like; while other things, again, without tormenting are fitted to comfort and soothe the languishing, as, for example, consolations, exhortations, discussions, and such things; in all these the supreme justice of God makes use sometimes even of wicked men, acting in ignorance, and sometimes of good men, acting intelligently. It is ours, accordingly, to desire in preference the better part, that we might attain our end

in your correction, not by contention, and strife, and persecutions, but by kindly consolation, by friendly exhortation, by quiet discussion; as it is written, "The servant of the Lord must not strive; but be gentle toward all men, apt to teach, patient; in meekness instructing those that oppose themselves." It is ours, I say, to desire to obtain this part in the work; it belongs to God to give what is good to those who desire it and ask for it.

Chapter 2. —Why the Manichæans Should Be More Gently Dealt with.

2. Let those rage against you who know not with what labor the truth is to be found and with what difficulty error is to be avoided. Let those rage against you who know not how rare and hard it is to overcome the fancies of the flesh by the serenity of a pious disposition. Let those rage against you who know not the difficulty of curing the eye of the inner man that he may gaze upon his Sun,—not that sun which you worship, and which shines with the brilliance of a heavenly body in the eyes of carnal men and of beasts,—but that of which it is written through the prophet, "The Sun of righteousness has arisen upon me;" and of which it is said in the gospel, "That was the true Light, which lighted every man that cometh into the world." Let those rage against you who know not with what sighs and groans the least particle of the knowledge of God is obtained. And, last of all, let those rage against you who have never been led astray in the same way that they see that you are.

Chapter 3. —Augustin Once a Manichæan.

3. For my part, I,—who, after much and long-continued bewilderment, attained at last, to the discovery of the simple truth, which is learned without being recorded in any fanciful legend; who, unhappy that I was, barely succeeded, by God's help, in refuting the vain imaginations of my mind, gathered from theories and errors of various kinds; who so late sought the cure of my mental obscuration, in compliance with the call and the tender persuasion of the all-merciful Physician; who long wept that the immutable and inviolable Existence would vouchsafe to convince me inwardly of Himself, in harmony with the testimony of the sacred books; by whom, in fine, all those fictions which have such a firm hold on you, from your long familiarity with them, were diligently examined, and attentively heard, and too easily believed, and commended at every opportunity to the belief of others, and defended against opponents with determination and boldness,—I can on no account rage against you; for I must bear with you now as formerly I had to bear with myself, and I must be as patient towards you as my associates were with me, when I went madly and blindly astray in your beliefs.

4. On the other hand, all must allow that you owe it to me, in return, to lay aside all arrogance on your part too, that so you may be the more disposed to gentleness, and may not oppose me in a hostile spirit, to your own hurt. Let neither of us assert that he has found truth; let us seek it as if it were unknown to us both. For truth can be sought with zeal and unanimity if by no rash presumption it is believed to have been already found and ascertained. But if I cannot induce you to grant me this, at least allow

me to suppose myself a stranger now for the first time hearing you, for the first time examining your doctrines. I think my demand a just one. And it must be laid down as an understood thing that I am not to join you in your prayers, or in holding conventicles, or in taking the name of Manichæus, unless you give me a clear explanation, without any obscurity, of all matters touching the salvation of the soul.

Chapter 4. —Proofs of the Catholic Faith.

5. For in the Catholic Church, not to speak of the purest wisdom, to the knowledge of which a few spiritual men attain in this life, so as to know it, in the scantiest measure, indeed, because they are but men, still without any uncertainty (since the rest of the multitude derive their entire security not from acuteness of intellect, but from simplicity of faith,)—not to speak of this wisdom, which you do not believe to be in the Catholic Church, there are many other things which most justly keep me in her bosom. The consent of peoples and nations keeps me in the Church; so does her authority, inaugurated by miracles, nourished by hope, enlarged by love, established by age. The succession of priests keeps me, beginning from the very seat of the Apostle Peter, to whom the Lord, after His resurrection, gave it in charge to feed His sheep, down to the present episcopate. And so, lastly, does the name itself of Catholic, which, not without reason, amid so many heresies, the Church has thus retained; so that, though all heretics wish to be called Catholics, yet when a stranger asks where the Catholic Church meets, no heretic will venture to point to his own chapel or house. Such then in number and importance are

the precious ties belonging to the Christian name which keep a believer in the Catholic Church, as it is right they should, though from the slowness of our understanding, or the small attainment of our life, the truth may not yet fully disclose itself. But with you, where there is none of these things to attract or keep me, the promise of truth is the only thing that comes into play. Now if the truth is so clearly proved as to leave no possibility of doubt, it must be set before all the things that keep me in the Catholic Church; but if there is only a promise without any fulfillment, no one shall move me from the faith which binds my mind with ties so many and so strong to the Christian religion.

Chapter 5. —Against the Title of the Epistle of Manichæus.

6. Let us see then what Manichæus teaches me; and particularly let us examine that treatise which he calls the Fundamental Epistle, in which almost all that you believe is contained. For in that unhappy time when we read it we were in your opinion enlightened. The epistle begins thus: —"Manichæus, an apostle of Jesus Christ, by the providence of God the Father. These are wholesome words from the perennial and living fountain." Now, if you please, patiently give heed to my inquiry. I do not believe Manichæus to be an apostle of Christ. Do not, I beg of you, be enraged and begin to curse. For you know that it is my rule to believe none of your statements without consideration. Therefore I ask, who is this Manichæus? You will reply, An apostle of Christ. I do not believe it. Now you are at a loss what to say or do; for you promised to give knowledge of the truth, and here

you are forcing me to believe what I have no knowledge of. Perhaps you will read the gospel to me, and will attempt to find there a testimony to Manichæus. But should you meet with a person not yet believing the gospel, how would you reply to him were he to say, I do not believe? For my part, I should not believe the gospel except as moved by the authority of the Catholic Church. So when those on whose authority I have consented to believe in the gospel tell me not to believe in Manichæus, how can I but consent? Take your choice. If you say, Believe the Catholics: their advice to me is to put no faith in you; so that, believing them, I am precluded from believing you;—If you say, Do not believe the Catholics: you cannot fairly use the gospel in bringing me to faith in Manichæus; for it was at the command of the Catholics that I believed the gospel;—Again, if you say, You were right in believing the Catholics when they praised the gospel, but wrong in believing their vituperation of Manichæus: do you think me such a fool as to believe or not to believe as you like or dislike, without any reason? It is therefore fairer and safer by far for me, having in one instance put faith in the Catholics, not to go over to you, till, instead of bidding me believe, you make me understand something in the clearest and most open manner. To convince me, then, you must put aside the gospel. If you keep to the gospel, I will keep to those who commanded me to believe the gospel; and, in obedience to them, I will not believe you at all. But if haply you should succeed in finding in the gospel an incontrovertible testimony to the apostleship of Manichæus, you will weaken my regard for the authority of the Catholics who bid me not to believe you; and the effect of that will be, that I shall no longer be able to believe the gospel either, for it was through the Catholics that I got my faith in it; and so, whatever you bring from the gospel will no longer have any weight with me. Wherefore, if no clear proof of the apostleship of Manichæus is found in the gospel, I will believe the Catholics rather than you. But if you read thence some passage clearly in favor of Manichæus, I will believe neither them nor you: not them, for they lied to me about you; nor you, for you quote to me that Scripture which I had believed on the authority of those liars. But far be it that I should not believe the gospel; for believing it, I find no way of believing you too. For the names of the apostles, as there recorded, do not include the name of Manichæus. And who the successor of Christ's betrayer was we read in the Acts of the Apostles; which book I must needs believe if I believe the gospel, since both writings alike Catholic authority commends to me. The same book contains the well-known narrative of the calling and apostleship of Paul. Read me now, if you can, in the gospel where Manichæus is called an apostle, or in any other book in which I have professed to believe. Will you read the passage where the Lord promised the Holy Spirit as a Paraclete, to the apostles? Concerning which passage, behold how many and how great are the things that restrain and deter me from believing in Manichæus.

Chapter 6. —Why Manichæus Called Himself an Apostle of Christ.

7. For I am at a loss to see why this epistle begins, "Manichæus, an apostle of Jesus Christ," and not Paraclete, an apostle of Jesus Christ. Or if the Paraclete sent by Christ sent Manichæus, why do we read,

"Manichæus, an apostle of Jesus Christ," instead of Manichæus, an apostle of the Paraclete? If you say that it is Christ Himself who is the Holy Spirit, you contradict the very Scripture, where the Lord says, "And I will send you another Paraclete." Again, if you justify your putting of Christ's name, not because it is Christ Himself who is also the Paraclete, but because they are both of the same substance, —that is, not because they are one person, but one existence [non quia unus est, sed quia unum sunt], — Paul too might have used the words, Paul, an apostle of God the Father; for the Lord said, "I and the Father are one." Paul nowhere uses these words; nor does any of the apostles write himself an apostle of the Father. Why then this new fashion? Does it not savor of trickery of some kind or other? For if he thought it made no difference, why did he not for the sake of variety in some epistles call himself an apostle of Christ, and in others of the Paraclete? But in everyone that I know of, he writes, of Christ; and not once, of the Paraclete. What do we supposed to be the reason of this, but that pride, the mother of all heretics, impelled the man to desire to seem to have been sent by the Paraclete, but to have been taken into so close a relation as to get the name of Paraclete himself? As the man Jesus Christ was not sent by the Son of God, that is, the power and wisdom of God—by which all things were made, but, according to the Catholic faith, was taken into such a relation as to be Himself the Son of God—that is, that in Himself the wisdom of God was displayed in the healing of sinners,—so Manichæus wished it to be thought that he was so taken up by the Holy Spirit, whom Christ promised, that we are henceforth to understand that the names Manichæus and Holy Spirit alike signify the apostle of Jesus Christ,—that is, one sent by Jesus Christ, who promised to send him. Singular audacity this! and unutterable sacrilege!

Chapter 7. —In What Sense the Followers of Manichæus Believe Him to Be the Holy Spirit.

8. Besides, you should explain how it is that, while the Father, Son, and Holy Spirit are united in equality of nature, as you also acknowledge, you are not ashamed to speak of Manichæus, a man taken into union with the Holy Spirit, as born of ordinary generation; and yet you shrink from believing that the man taken into union with the only-begotten Wisdom of God was born of a Virgin. If human flesh, if generation [concubitus viri], if the womb of a woman could not contaminate the Holy Spirit, how could the Virgin's womb contaminate the Wisdom of God? This Manichæus, then, who boasts of a connection with the Holy Spirit, and of being spoken of in the gospel, must produce his claim to either of these two things, —that he was sent by the Spirit, or that he was taken into union with the Spirit. If he was sent, let him call himself the apostle of the Paraclete; if taken into union, let him allow that He whom the only-begotten Son took upon Himself had a human mother, since he admits a human father as well as mother in the case of one taken up by the Holy Spirit. Let him believe that the Word of God was not defiled by the virgin womb of Mary, since he exhorts us to believe that the Holy Spirit could not be defiled by the married life of his parents. But if you say that Manichæus was united to the Spirit, not in the womb or before conception, but after his birth, still you must admit that he had a fleshly nature derived from man and woman. And since you are not afraid to speak of the

blood and the bodily substance of Manichæus as coming from ordinary generation, or of the internal impurities contained in his flesh, and hold that the Holy Spirit, who took on Himself, as you believe, this human being, was not contaminated by all those things, why should I shrink from speaking of the Virgin's womb and body undefiled, and not rather believe that the Wisdom of God in union with the human being in his mother's flesh still remained free from stain and pollution? Wherefore, as, whether your Manichæus professes to be sent by or to be united with the Paraclete, neither statement can hold good, I am on my guard, and refuse to believe either in his mission or in his susception.

Chapter 8. —The Festival of the Birth-Day of Manichæus.

9. In adding the words, "by the providence of God the Father," what else did Manichæus design but that, having got the name of Jesus Christ, whose apostle he calls himself, and of God the Father, by whose providence he says he was sent by the Son, we should believe himself, as the Holy Spirit, to be the third person? His words are: "Manichæus, an apostle of Jesus Christ, by the providence of God the Father." The Holy Spirit is not named, though He ought specially to have been named by one who quotes to us in favor of his apostleship the promise of the Paraclete, that he may prevail upon ignorant people by the authority of the gospel. In reply to this, you of course say that in the name of the Apostle Manichæus we have the name of the Holy Spirit, the Paraclete, because He condescended to come into Manichæus. Why then, I ask again, should you cry out

against the doctrine of the Catholic Church, that He in whom divine Wisdom came was born of a virgin, when you do not scruple to affirm the birth by ordinary generation of him in whom you say the Holy Spirit came? I cannot but suspect that this Manichæus, who uses the name of Christ to gain access to the minds of the ignorant, wished to be worshipped instead of Christ Himself. I will state briefly the reason of this conjecture. At the time when I was a student of your doctrines, to my frequent inquiries why it was that the Paschal feast of the Lord was celebrated generally with no interest, though sometimes there were a few languid worshippers, but no watchings, no prescription of any unusual fast,—in a word, no special ceremony,—while great honor is paid to your Bema, that is, the day on which Manichæus was killed, when you have a platform with fine steps, covered with precious cloth, placed conspicuously so as to face the votaries,—the reply was, that the day to observe was the day of the passion of him who really suffered, and that Christ, who was not born, but appeared to human eyes in an unreal semblance of flesh, only feigned suffering, without really bearing it. Is it not deplorable, that men who wish to be called Christians are afraid of a virgin's womb as likely to defile the truth, and yet are not afraid of falsehood? But to go back to the point, who that pays attention can help suspecting that the intention of Manichæus in denying Christ's being born of a woman, and having a human body, was that His passion, the time of which is now a great festival all over the world, might not be observed by the believers in himself, so as to lessen the devotion of the solemn commemoration which he wished in honor of the day of his own death? For to us it was a great attraction in the feast of the Bema that it was held during Pascha, since we used all the more earnestly to desire that festal day [the Bema], that the other which was formerly most sweet had been withdrawn.

Chapter 9. —When the Holy Spirit Was Sent.

10. Perhaps you will say to me, When, then, did the Paraclete promised by the Lord come? About this, had I nothing else to believe on the subject, I should rather look for the Paraclete as still to come, than allow that He came in Manichæus. But seeing that the advent of the Holy Spirit is narrated with perfect clearness in the Acts of the Apostles, where is the necessity of my so gratuitously running the risk of believing heretics? For in the Acts it is written as follows: "The former treatise have we made, O Theophilus, of all that Jesus began both to do and teach, in the day in which He chose the apostles by the Holy Spirit, and commanded them to preach the gospel. By those to whom He showed Himself alive after His passion by many proofs in the daytime, He was seen forty days, teaching concerning the kingdom of God. And how He conversed with them, and commanded them that they should not depart from Jerusalem, but wait for the promise of the Father, which, saith He, ye have heard of me. For John indeed baptized with water, but ye shall begin to be baptized with the Holy Spirit, whom also ye shall receive after not many days, that is, at Pentecost. When they had come, they asked him, saying, Lord, wilt Thou at this time manifest Thyself? And when will be the kingdom of Israel? And He said unto them, No one can know the time which the Father hath put in His own power. But ye shall receive the power of the Holy Ghost coming upon you, and ye shall be witnesses unto me both

in Jerusalem, and in all Judæa, and in Samaria, and unto the uttermost part of the earth." Behold you have here the Lord reminding His disciples of the promise of the Father, which they had heard from His mouth, of the coming of the Holy Spirit. Let us now see when He was sent; for shortly after we read as follows: "And when the day of Pentecost was fully come, they were all with one accord in one place. And suddenly there came a sound from heaven, as of a rushing mighty wind, and it filled all the house where they were sitting. And there appeared unto them cloven tongues, like as of fire, and it sat upon each of them. And they were all filled with the Holy Ghost, and began to speak with other tongues, as the Spirit gave them utterance. And there were dwelling at Jerusalem Jews, devout men, out of every nation under heaven. And when the sound was heard, the multitude came together, and were confounded, because every man heard them speak in his own language. And they were all amazed, and marveled, saying one to another, Are not all these which speak Galileans? and how heard we every man in our own tongue, wherein we were born? Parthians, and Medes, and Elamites, and the dwellers in Mesopotamia, in Armenia, and in Cappadocia, in Pontus, Asia, Phrygia, and Pamphylia, in Egypt, and in the regions of Africa about Cyrene, and strangers of Rome, Jews, natives, Cretes, and Arabians, they heard them speak in their own tongues the wonderful works of God. And they were all amazed, and were in doubt because what had happened, saying, What means this? But others, mocking, said, These men are full of new wine." You see when the Holy Spirit came. What more do you wish? If the Scriptures are credible, should not I believe most readily in these Acts, which have the strongest testimony in their support, and which have had the advantage of becoming generally known, and of being handed down and of being publicly taught along with the gospel itself, which contains the promise of the Holy Spirit, which also we believe? On reading, then, these Acts of the Apostles, which stand, as regards authority, on a level with the gospel, I find that not only was the Holy Spirit promised to these true apostles, but that He was also sent so manifestly, that no room was left for errors on this subject.

Chapter 10. —The Holy Spirit Twice Given.

11. For the glorification of our Lord among men is His resurrection from the dead and His ascension to heaven. For it is written in the Gospel according to John: "The Holy Ghost was not yet given, because that Jesus was not yet glorified." Now if the reason why He was not given was that Jesus was not yet glorified, He was given immediately on the glorification of Jesus. And since that glorification was twofold, as regards man and as regards God, twice also was the Holy Spirit given: once, when, after His resurrection from the dead, He breathed on the face of His disciples, saying, "Receive ye the Holy Ghost;" and again, ten days after His ascension to heaven. This number ten signifies perfection; for to the number seven which embraces all created things, is added the trinity of the Creator. On these things there is much pious and sober discourse among spiritual men. But I must keep to my point; for my business at present is not to teach you, which you might think presumptuous, but to take the part of an inquirer, and learn from you, as I tried to do for nine years without success. Now, therefore, I have a document to believe on the subject of the Holy

Spirit's advent; and if you bid me not to believe this document, as your usual advice is not to believe ignorantly, without consideration, much less will I believe your documents. Away, then, with all books, and disclose the truth with logical clearness, so as to leave no doubt in my mind; or bring forward books where I shall find not an imperious demand for my belief, but a trustworthy statement of what I may learn. Perhaps you say this epistle is also of this character. Let me, then, no longer stop at the threshold: let us see the contents.

Chapter 11. —Manichæus Promises Truth, But Does Not Make Good His Word.

12. "These," he says, "are wholesome words from the perennial and living fountain; and whoever shall have heard them, and shall have first believed them, and then shall have observed the truths they set forth, shall never suffer death, but shall enjoy eternal life in glory. For he is to be judged truly blessed who has been instructed in this divine knowledge, by which he is made free and shall abide in everlasting life." And this, as you see, is a promise of truth, but not the bestowal of it. And you yourselves can easily see that any errors whatever might be dressed up in this fashion, so as under cover of a showy exterior to steal in unawares into the minds of the ignorant. Were he to say, These are pestiferous words from a poisonous fountain; and whoever shall have heard them, and shall have first believed them, and then have observed what they set forth, shall never be restored to life, but shall suffer a woeful death as a criminal: for assuredly he is to be pronounced miserable who falls into this infernal error, in which he will sink so as to abide in

everlasting torments;—were he to say this, he would say the truth; but instead of gaining any readers for his book, he would excite the greatest aversion in the minds of all into whose hands the book might come. Let us then pass on to what follows; nor let us be deceived by words which may be used alike by good and bad, by learned and unlearned. What, then, comes next?

13. "May the peace," he says, "of the invisible God, and the knowledge of the truth, be with the holy and beloved brethren who both believe and also yield obedience to the divine precepts." Amen, say we. For the prayer is a most amiable and commendable one. Only we must bear in mind that these words might be used by false teachers as well as by good ones. So, if he said nothing more than this, all might safely read and embrace it. Nor should I disapprove of what follows: "May also the right hand of light protect you, and deliver you from every hostile assault, and from the snares of the world." In fact, I have no fault to find with the beginning of this epistle, till we come to the main subject of it. For I wish not to spend time on minor points. Now, then, for this writer's plain statement of what is to be expected from him.

Chapter 12. —The Wild Fancies of Manichæus. The Battle Before the Constitution of the World.

14. "Of that matter," he says, "beloved brother of Patticus, of which you told me, saying that you desired to know the manner of the birth of Adam and Eve, whether they were produced by a word or sprung from matter, I will answer you as is fit. For in various writings and narratives we find different assertions made and different descriptions given by many authors. Now the real truth

on the subject is unknown to all peoples, even to those who have long and frequently treated of it. For had they arrived at a clear knowledge of the generation of Adam and Eve, they would not have remained liable to corruption and death." Here, then, is a promise to us of clear knowledge of this matter, so that we shall not be liable to corruption and death. And if this does not suffice, see what follows: "Necessarily," he says, "many things have to be said by way of preface, before a discovery of this mystery free from all uncertainty can be made." This is precisely what I asked for, to have such evidence of the truth as to free my knowledge of it from all uncertainty. And even were the promise not made by this writer himself, it was proper for me to demand and to insist upon this, so that no opposition should make me ashamed of becoming a Manichæan from a Catholic Christian, in view of such a gain as that of perfectly clear and certain truth. Now, then, let us hear what he has to state.

15. "Accordingly," he says, "hear first, if you please, what happened before the constitution of the world, and how the battle was carried on, that you may be able to distinguish the nature of light from that of darkness." Such are the utterly false and incredible statements which this writer makes. Who can believe that any battle was fought before the constitution of the world? And even supposing it credible, we wish now to get something to know, not to believe. For to say that the Persians and Scythians long ago fought with one another is a credible statement; but while we believe it when we read or hear it, we cannot know it as a fact of experience or as a truth of the understanding. So, then, as I would repudiate any such statement because I have been

promised something, not that I must believe on authority, but that I shall understand without any ambiguity; still less will I receive statements which are not only uncertain, but incredible. But what if he have some evidence to make these things clear and intelligible? Let us hear, then, if we can, what follows with all possible patience and forbearance.

Chapter 13. —Two Opposite Substances. The Kingdom of Light. Manichæus Teaches Uncertainties Instead of Certainties.

16. "In the beginning, then," he says, "these two substances were divided. The empire of light was held by God the Father, who is perpetual in holy origin, magnificent in virtue, true in His very nature, ever rejoicing in His own eternity, possessing in Himself wisdom and the vital senses, by which He also includes the twelve members of His light, which are the plentiful resources of his kingdom. Also in each of His members are stored thousands of untold and priceless treasures. But the Father Himself, chief in praise, incomprehensible in greatness, has united to Himself happy and glorious worlds, incalculable in number and duration, along with which this holy and illustrious Father and Progenitor resides, no poverty or infirmity being admitted in His magnificent realms. And these matchless realms are so founded on the region of light and bliss, that no one can ever move or disturb them."

17. Where is the proof of all this? And where did Manichæus learn it? Do not frighten me with the name of the Paraclete. For, in the first place, I have come not to put faith in unknown things, but to get the knowledge of

undoubted truths, according to the caution enjoined on me by yourselves. For you know how bitterly you taunt those who believe without consideration. And what is more, this writer, who here begins to tell of very doubtful things, himself promised a little before to give complete and well-grounded knowledge.

Chapter 14. —Manichæus Promises the Knowledge of Undoubted Things, and Then Demands Faith in Doubtful Things.

In the next place, if faith is what is required of me, I should prefer to keep to the Scripture, which tells me that the Holy Spirit came and inspired the apostles, to whom the Lord had promised to send Him. You must therefore prove, either that what Manichæus says is true, and so make clear to me what I am unable to believe; or that Manichæus is the Holy Spirit, and so lead me to believe in what you cannot make clear. For I profess the Catholic faith, and by it I expect to attain certain knowledge. Since, then, you try to overthrow my faith, you must supply me with certain knowledge, if you can, that you may convict me of having adopted my present belief without consideration. You make two distinct propositions, —one when you say that the speaker is the Holy Spirit, and another when you say that what the speaker teaches is evidently true. I might fairly ask undeniable proof for both propositions. But I am not greedy and require to be convinced only of one. Prove this person to be the Holy Spirit, and I will believe what he says to be true, even without understanding it; or prove that what he says is true, and I will believe him to be the Holy Spirit, even without evidence. Could anything be fairer or kinder than this? But you cannot prove either one or other of these propositions. You can find nothing better than to praise your own faith and ridicule mine. So, after having in my turn praised my belief and ridiculed yours, what result do you think we shall arrive at as regards our judgment and our conduct, but to part company with those who promise the knowledge of indubitable things, and then demand from us faith in doubtful things? while we shall follow those who invite us to begin with believing what we cannot yet fully perceive, that, strengthened by this very faith, we may come into a position to know what we believe by the inward illumination and confirmation of our minds, due no longer to men, but to God Himself.

18. And as I have asked this writer to prove these things to me, I ask him now where he learned them himself. If he replies that they were revealed to him by the Holy Spirit, and that his mind was divinely enlightened that he might know them to be certain and evident, he himself points to the distinction between knowing and believing. The knowledge is his to whom these things are fully made known as proved; but in the case of those who only hear his account of these things, there is no knowledge imparted, but only a believing acquiescence required. Whoever thoughtlessly yields this becomes a Manichæan, not by knowing undoubted truth, but by believing doubtful statements. Such were we when in our inexperienced youth we were deceived. Instead, therefore, of promising knowledge, or clear evidence, or the settlement of the question free from all uncertainty, Manichæus ought to have said that these things were clearly proved to him, but that those who hear his account of them must believe him without evidence. But were he

to say this, who would not reply to him, If I must believe without knowing, why should I not prefer to believe those things which have a widespread notoriety from the consent of learned and unlearned, and which among all nations are established by the weightiest authority? From fear of having this said to him, Manichæus bewilders the inexperienced by first promising the knowledge of certain truths, and then demanding faith in doubtful things. And then, if he is asked to make it plain that these things have been proved to himself, he fails again, and bids us believe this too. Who can tolerate such imposture and arrogance?

Chapter 15. —The Doctrine of Manichæus Not Only Uncertain, But False. His Absurd Fancy of a Land and Race of Darkness Bordering on the Holy Region and the Substance of God. The Error, First of All, of Giving to the Nature of God Limits and Borders, as If God Were a Material Substance, Having Extension in Space.

19. What if I shall have shown, with the help of God and of our Lord, that this writer's statements are false as well as uncertain? What more unfortunate thing can be found than that superstition which not only fails to impart the knowledge and the truth which it promises, but also teaches what is directly opposed to knowledge and truth? This will appear more clearly from what follows: "In one direction on the border of this bright and holy land there was a land of darkness deep and vast in extent, where abode fiery bodies, destructive races. Here was boundless darkness, flowing from the same source in immeasurable abundance, with the productions properly belonging to it. Beyond this were muddy turbid waters with their inhabitants; and inside of them winds terrible

and violent with their prince and their progenitors. Then again a fiery region of destruction, with its chiefs and peoples. And similarly inside of this a race full of smoke and gloom, where abode the dreadful prince and chief of all, having around him innumerable princes, himself the mind and source of them all. Such are the five natures of the pestiferous land."

20. To speak of God as an aerial or even as an ethereal body is absurd in the view of all who, with a clear mind, possessing some measure of discernment, can perceive the nature of wisdom and truth as not extended or scattered in space, but as great, and imparting greatness without material size, nor confined more or less in any direction, but throughout co-extensive with the Father of all, nor having one thing here and another there, but everywhere perfect, everywhere present.

Chapter 16. —The Soul, Though Mutable, Has No Material Form. It is All Present in Every Part of the Body.

But why speak of truth and wisdom which surpass all the powers of the soul, when the nature of the soul itself, which is known to be mutable, still has no kind of material extension in space? For whatever consists of any kind of gross matter must necessarily be divisible into parts, having one in one place, and another in another. Thus, the finger is less than the whole hand, and one finger is less than two; and there is one place for this finger, and another for that, and another for the rest of the hand. And this applies not to organized bodies only, but also to the earth, each part of which has its own place, so that one cannot be where the other is. So in moisture, the smaller quantity occupies a smaller space, and the larger quantity a larger space; and one part is at the bottom of the cup, and another part near the mouth. So in air, each part has its own place; and it is impossible for the air in this house to have along with itself, in the same house at the same moment, the air that the neighbors have. And even about light itself, one part pours through one window, and another through another; and a greater through the larger, and a smaller through the smaller. Nor, in fact, can there be any bodily substance, whether celestial or terrestrial, whether aerial or moist, which is not less in part than in whole, or which can possibly have one part in the place of another at the same time; but, having one thing in one place and another in another, its extension in space is a substance which has distinct limits and parts, or, so to speak, sections. The nature of the soul, on the other hand, though we leave out of account its power of perceiving truth, and consider only its inferior power of giving unity to the body, and of sensation in the body, does not appear to have any material extension in space. For it is all present in each separate part of its body when it is all present in any sensation. There is not a smaller part in the finger, and a larger in the arm, as the bulk of the finger is less than that of the arm; but the quantity everywhere is the same, for the whole is present everywhere. For when the finger is touched, the whole mind feels, though the sensation is not through the whole body. No part of the mind is unconscious of the touch, which proves the presence of the whole. And yet it is not so present in the finger or in the sensation as to abandon the rest of the body, or to gather itself up into the one place where the sensation occurs. For when it is all present in the sensation in a finger, if another part, say the foot, be touched, it does not fail to be all present in this sensation too: so that at the same moment it is all present in different places, without leaving one in order to be in the other, and without having one part in one, and another in the other; but by this power showing itself to be all present at the same moment in separate places. Since it is all present in the sensations of these places, it proves that it is not bound by the conditions of space.

Chapter 17. —The Memory Contains the Ideas of Places of the Greatest Size.

Again, if we consider the mind's power of remembering not the objects of the intellect, but material objects, such as we see brutes also remembering (for cattle find their way without mistake in familiar places, and animals return to their cribs, and dogs recognize the persons of their masters, and when asleep they often growl, or break out into a bark, which could not be unless their mind retained the images of things before seen or perceived by some bodily sense), who can conceive rightly where these images are contained, where they are kept, or where they are formed? If, indeed, these images were no larger than the size of our body, it might be said that the mind shapes and retains them in the bodily space which contains itself. But while the body occupies a small material space, the mind revolves images of vast extent, of heaven and earth, with no want of room, though they come and go in crowds; so that clearly, the mind is not diffused through space: for instead of being contained in images of the largest spaces, it rather contains them; not, however, in any material receptacle, but by a mysterious faculty or power, by which it can increase or diminish them, can contract them within narrow limits, or expand them indefinitely, can arrange or disarrange them at pleasure, can multiply them or reduce them to a few or to one.

Chapter 18. —The Understanding Judges of the Truth of Things, and of Its Own Action.

What, then, must be said of the power of perceiving truth, and of making a vigorous resistance against these very images which take their shape from impressions on the bodily senses, when they are opposed to the truth? This power discerns the difference between, to take a particular example, the true Carthage and its own imaginary one, which it changes as it pleases with perfect ease. It shows that the countless worlds of Epicurus, in which his fancy roamed without restraint, are due to the same power of imagination, and, not to multiply examples, that we get from the same source that land of light, with its boundless extent, and the five dens of the race of darkness, with their inmates, in which the fancies of Manichæus have dared to usurp for themselves the name of truth. What then is this power which discerns these things? Clearly, whatever its extent may be, it is greater than all these things, and is conceived of without any such material images. Find, if you can, space for this power; give it a material extension; provide it with a body of huge size. Assuredly if you think well, you cannot. For of everything of this corporeal nature your mind forms an opinion as to its divisibility, and you make of such things one part greater and another less, as much as you like; while that by which you form a judgment of these things you perceive to be above them, not in local loftiness of place, but in dignity of power.

Chapter 19. —If the Mind Has No Material Extension, Much Less Has God.

21. So then, if the mind, so liable to change, whether from a multitude of dissimilar desires, or from feelings varying according to the abundance or the want of desirable things, or from these endless sports of the fancy, or from forgetfulness and remembrance, or from learning and ignorance; if the mind, I say, exposed to frequent change from these and the like causes, is perceived to be without any local or material extension, and to have a vigor of action which surmounts these material conditions, what must we think or conclude of God Himself, who remains superior to all intelligent beings in His freedom from perturbation and from change, giving to everyone what is due? Him the mind dares to express more easily than to see; and the clearer the sight, the less is the power of expression. And yet this God, if, as the Manichæan fables are constantly asserting, He were limited in extension in one direction and unlimited in others, could be measured by so many subdivisions or fractions of greater or less size, as everyone might fancy; so that, for example, a division of the extent of two feet would be less by eight parts than one of ten feet. For this is the property of all natures which have extension in space, and therefore cannot be all in one place. But even with the mind this is not the case; and this degrading and perverted idea of the mind is found among people who are unfit for such investigations.

Chapter 20. —Refutation of the Absurd Idea of Two Territories.

22. But perhaps, instead of thus addressing carnal minds, we should rather descend to the views of those who either dare not or are as yet unfit to turn from the consideration of material things to the study of an immaterial and spiritual nature, and who thus are unable to reflect upon their own power of reflection, so as to see how it forms a judgment of material extension without itself possessing it. Let us descend then to these material ideas, and let us ask in what direction, and on what border of the shining and sacred territory, to use the expressions of Manichæus, was the region of darkness? For he speaks of one direction and border, without saying which, whether the right or the left. In any case, it is clear that to speak of one side implies that there is another. But where there are three or more sides, either the figure is bounded in all directions, or if it extends infinitely in one direction, still it must be limited in the directions where it has sides. If, then, on one side of the region of light there was the race of darkness, what bounded it on the other side or sides? The Manichæans say nothing in reply to this; but when pressed, they say that on the other sides the region of light, as they call it, is infinite, that is, extends throughout boundless space. They do not see, what is plain to the dullest understanding, that in that case there could be no sides? For the sides are where it is bounded. What, then, he says, though there are no sides? But what you said of one direction or side, implied of necessity the existence of another direction and side, or other directions and sides. For if there was only one side, you should have said, on the side, not on one side; as in reference to our

body we say properly, By one eye, because there is another; or on one breast, because there is another. But if we spoke of a thing as being on one nose, or one navel, we should be ridiculed by learned and unlearned, since there is only one. But I do not insist on words, for you may have used one in the sense of the only one.

Chapter 21. —This Region of Light Must Be Material If It is Joined to the Region of Darkness. The Shape of the Region of Darkness Joined to the Region of Light.

What, then, bordered on the side of the region which you call shining and sacred? The region, you reply, of darkness. Do you then allow this latter region to have been material? Of course you must, since you assert that all bodies derive their origin from it. How then is it that, dull and carnal as you are, you do not see that unless both regions were material, they could not have their sides joined to one another? How could you ever be so blinded in mind as to say that only the region of darkness was material, and that the so-called region of light was immaterial and spiritual? My good friends, let us open our eyes for once, and see, now that we are told of it, what is most obvious, that two regions cannot be joined at their sides unless both are material.

23. Or if we are too dull and stupid to see this, let us hear whether the region of darkness too has one side, and is boundless in the other directions, like the region of light. They do not hold this from fear of making it seem equal to God. Accordingly they make it boundless in depth and in length; but upwards, above it, they maintain that there is an infinity of empty space. And lest this

region should appear to be a fraction equal in amount to half of that representing the region of light, they narrow it also on two sides. As if, to give the simplest illustration, a piece of bread were made into four squares, three white and one black; then suppose the three white pieces joined as one, and conceive them as infinite upwards and downwards, and backwards in all directions: this represents the Manichæan region of light. Then conceive the black square infinite downwards and backwards, but with infinite emptiness above it: this is their region of darkness. But these are secrets which they disclose to very eager and anxious inquirers.

Chapter 22. —The Form of the Region of Light the Worse of the Two.

Well, then, if this is so, the region of darkness is clearly touched on two sides by the region of light. And if it is touched on two sides, it must touch on two. So much for its being on one side, as we were told before.
24. And what an unseemly appearance is this of the region of light! —like a cloven arch, with a black wedge inserted below, bounded only in the direction of the cleft, and having a void space interposed where the boundless emptiness stretches above the region of darkness. Indeed, the form of the region of darkness is better than that of the region of light: for the former cleaves, the latter is cloven; the former fills the gap which is made in the latter; the former has no void in it, while the latter is undefined in all directions, except that where it is filled up by the wedge of darkness. In an ignorant and greedy notion of giving more honor to a number of pans than to a single one, so that the region of light should

have six, three upwards and three downwards, they have made this region be split up, instead of sundering the other. For, according to this figure, though there may be no commixture of darkness with light, there is certainly penetration.

Chapter 23. —The Anthropomorphites Not So Bad as the Manichæans.

25. Compare, now, not spiritual men of the Catholic faith, whose mind, as far as is possible in this life, perceives that the divine substance and nature has no material extension, and has no shape bounded by lines, but the carnal and weak of our faith, who, when they hear the members of the body used figuratively, as, when God's eyes or ears are spoken of, are accustomed, in the license of fancy, to picture God to themselves in a human form; compare these with the Manichæans, whose custom it is to make known their silly stories to anxious inquirers as if they were great mysteries: and consider who have the most allowable and respectable ideas of God, —those who think of Him as having a human form which is the most excellent of its kind, or those who think of Him as having boundless material extension, yet not in all directions, but with three parts infinite and solid, while in one part He is cloven, with an empty void, and with undefined space above, while the region of darkness is inserted wedge-like below. Or perhaps the proper expression is, that He is unconfined above in His own nature, but encroached on below by a hostile nature. I join with you in laughing at the folly of carnal men, unable as yet to form spiritual conceptions, who think of God as having a human form. Do you too join me, if you

can, in laughing at those whose unhappy conceptions represent God as having a shape cloven or cut in such an unseemly and unbecoming way, with such an empty gap above, and such a dishonorable curtailment below. Besides, there is this difference, that these carnal people, who think of God as having a human form, if they are content to be nourished with milk from the breast of the Catholic Church, and do not rush headlong into rash opinions, but cultivate in the Church the pious habit of inquiry, and there ask that they may receive, and knock that it may be opened to them, begin to understand spiritually the figures and parables of the Scriptures, and gradually to perceive that the divine energies are suitably set forth under the name, sometimes of ears, sometimes of eyes, sometimes of hands or feet, or even of wings and feathers a shield too, and sword, and helmet, and all the other innumerable things. And the more progress they make in this understanding, the more are they confirmed as Catholics. The Manichæans, on the other hand, when they abandon their material fancies, cease to be Manichæans. For this is the chief and special point in their praises of Manichæus, that the divine mysteries which were taught figuratively in books from ancient times were kept for Manichæus, who was to come last, to solve and demonstrate; and so after him no other teacher will come from God, for he has said nothing in figures or parables, but has explained ancient sayings of that kind, and has himself taught in plain, simple terms. Therefore, when the Manichæans hear these words of their founder, on one side and border of the shining and sacred region was the region of darkness, they have no interpretations to fall back on. Wherever they turn, the wretched bondage of their own fancies brings them upon clefts or sudden stoppages and joinings or sunderings of the most unseemly kind, which it would be shocking to believe as true of any immaterial nature, even though mutable, like the mind, not to speak of the immutable nature of God. And yet if I were unable to rise to higher things, and to bring my thoughts from the entanglement of false imaginations which are impressed on the memory by the bodily senses, into the freedom and purity of spiritual existence, how much better would it be to think of God as in the form of a man, than to fasten that wedge of darkness to His lower edge, and, for want of a covering for the boundless vacuity above to leave it void and unoccupied throughout infinite space! What notion could be worse than this? What darker error can be taught or imagined?

Chapter 24. —Of the Number of Natures in the Manichæan Fiction.

26. Again, I wish to know, when I read of God the Father and His kingdoms founded on the shining and happy region, whether the Father and His kingdoms, and the region, are all of the same nature and substance. If they are, then it is not another nature or sort of body of God which the wedge of the race of darkness cleaves and penetrates, which itself is an unspeakably revolting thing, but it is actually the very nature of God which undergoes this. Think of this, I beseech you: as you are men, think of it, and flee from it; and if by tearing open your breasts you can cast out by the roots such profane fancies from your faith, I pray you to do it. Or will you say that these three are not of one and the same nature, but that the Father is of one, the kingdoms of another, and the region

of another, so that each has a peculiar nature and substance, and that they are arranged according to their degree of excellence? If this is true, Manichæus should have taught that there are four natures, not two; or if the Father and the kingdoms have one nature, and the region only one of its own, he should have made three. Or if he made only two, because the region of darkness does not belong to God, in what sense does the region of light belong to God? For if it has a nature of its own, and if God neither generated nor made it, it does not belong to Him, and the seat of His kingdom is in what belongs to another. Or if it belongs to Him because of its vicinity, the region of darkness must do so too; for it not only borders on the region of light, but penetrates it so as to sever it in two. Again, if God generated it, it cannot have a separate nature. For what is generated by God must be what God is, as the Catholic Church believes of the only begotten Son. So you are brought back of necessity to that shocking and detestable profanity, that the wedge of darkness sunders not a region distinct and separate from God, but the very nature of God. Or if God did not generate, but make it, of what did He make it? Or if of Himself, what is this but to generate? If of some other nature, was this nature good or evil? If good, there must have been some good nature not belonging to God; which you will scarcely have the boldness to assert. If evil, the race of darkness cannot have been the only evil nature. Or did God take a part of that region and turn it into a region of light, in order to found His kingdom upon it? If He had, He would have taken the whole, and there would have been no evil nature left. If God, then, did not make the region of light of a substance distinct from His own, He must have made it of nothing.

Chapter 25. —Omnipotence Creates Good Things Differing in Degree. In Every Description Whatsoever of the Junction of the Two Regions There is Either Impropriety or Absurdity.

27. If, then, you are now convinced that God is able to create some good thing out of nothing, come into the Catholic Church, and learn that all the natures which God has created and founded in their order of excellence from the highest to the lowest are good, and some better than others; and that they were made of nothing, though God, their Maker, made use of His own wisdom as an instrument, so to speak, to give being to what was not, and that as far as it had being it might be good, and that the limitation of its being might show that it was not begotten by God, but made out of nothing. If you examine the matter, you will find nothing to keep you from agreeing to this. For you cannot make your region of light to be what God is, without making the dark section an infringement on the very nature of God. Nor can you say that it was generated by God, without being reduced to the same enormity, from the necessity of concluding that as begotten of God, it must be what God is. Nor can you say that it was distinct from Him, lest you should be forced to admit that God placed His kingdom in what did not belong to Him, and that there are three natures. Nor can you say that God made it of a substance distinct from His own, without making something good besides God, or something evil besides the race of darkness. It remains, therefore that you must confess that God made the region of light out of nothing: and you are unwilling to believe this; because if God could make out of nothing some great good which yet was inferior to

Himself, He could also, since He is good, and grudges no good, make another good inferior to the former, and again a third inferior to the second, and so on, in order down to the lowest good of created natures, so that the whole aggregate, instead of extending indefinitely without number or measure should have a fixed and definite consistency. Again, if you will not allow this either, that God made the region of light out of nothing, you will have no escape from the shocking profanities to which your opinions lead.

28. Perhaps, since the carnal imagination can fancy any shapes it likes, you might be able to devise some other form for the junction of the two regions, instead of presenting to the mind such a disagreeable and painful description as this, that the region of God, whether it be of the same nature as God or not, where at least God's kingdoms are founded, lies through immensity in such a huge mass that its members stretch loosely to an infinite extent, and that on their lower part that wedge of the region of darkness, itself of boundless size encroaches upon them. But whatever other form you contrive for the junction of these two regions, you cannot erase what Manichæus has written. I refer not to other treatises where a more particular description is given, —for perhaps, because they are in the hands of only a few, there might not be so much difficulty with them, —but to this Fundamental Epistle which we are now considering, with which all of you who are called enlightened are usually quite familiar. Here the words are: "On one side the border of the shining and sacred region was the region of darkness, deep and boundless in extent."

Chapter 26. —The Manichæans are Reduced to the Choice of a Tortuous, or Curved, or Straight Line of Junction. The Third Kind of Line Would Give Symmetry and Beauty Suitable to Both Regions.

What more is to be got? we have now heard what is on the border. Make what shape you please, draw any kind of lines you like, it is certain that the junction of this boundless mass of the region of darkness to the region of light must have been either by a straight line, or a curved, or a tortuous one. If the line of junction is tortuous the side of the region of light must also be tortuous; otherwise its straight side joined to a tortuous one would leave gaps of infinite depth, instead of having vacuity only above the land of darkness, as we were told before. And if there were such gaps, how much better it would have been for the region of light to have been still more distant, and to have had a greater vacuity between, so that the region of darkness might not touch it at all! Then there might have been such a gap of bottomless depth, that, on the rise of any mischief in that race, although the chiefs of darkness might have the foolhardy wish to cross over, they would fall headlong into the gap (for bodies cannot fly without air to support them); and as there is infinite space downwards, they could do no more harm, though they might live forever, for they would be forever falling. Again, if the line of junction was a curved one, the region of light must also have had the disfigurement of a curve to answer it. Or if the land of darkness were curved inwards like a theatre, there would be as much disfigurement in the corresponding line in the region of light. Or if the region of darkness had a curved line, and the region of light a straight one, they cannot have touched at all points. And certainly, as I said before, it would have been better if they had not touched, and if there was such a gap between that the regions might be kept distinctly separate, and that rash evildoers might fall headlong so as to be harmless. If, then, the line of junction was a straight one, there remain, of course, no more gaps or grooves, but, on the contrary, so perfect a junction as to make the greatest possible peace and harmony between the two regions. What more beautiful or more suitable than that one side should meet the other in a straight line, without bends or breaks to disturb the natural and permanent connection throughout endless space and endless duration? And even though there was a separation, the straight sides of both regions would be beautiful in themselves, as being straight; and besides, even despite an interval, their correspondence, as running parallel, though not meeting, would give a symmetry to both. With the addition of the junction, both regions become perfectly regular and harmonious; for nothing can be devised more beautiful in description or in conception than this junction of two straight lines.

Chapter 27. —The Beauty of the Straight Line Might Be Taken from the Region of Darkness Without Taking Anything from Its Substance. So Evil Neither Takes from Nor Adds to the Substance of the Soul. The Straightness of Its Side Would Be So Far a Good Bestowed on the Region of Darkness by God the Creator.

29. What is to be done with unhappy minds, perverse in error, and held fast by custom? These men do not know what they say when they say those things; for they do not consider. Listen to me; no one forces you, no

one quarrels with you, no one taunts you with past errors, unless someone who has not experienced the divine mercy in deliverance from error: all we desire is that the errors should some time or other be abandoned. Think a little without animosity or bitterness. We are all human beings: let us hate, not one another, but errors and lies. Think a little, I pray you. God of mercy, help them to think, and kindle in the minds of inquirers the true light. If anything is plain, is not this, that right is better than wrong? Give me, then, a calm and quiet answer to this, whether making crooked the right line of the region of darkness which joins on to the right line of the region of light, would not detract from its beauty. If you will not be dogged, you must confess that not only is beauty taken from it by its being made crooked, but also the beauty which it might have had from connection with the right line of the region of light. Is it the case, then, that in this loss of beauty, in which right is made crooked, and harmony becomes discord, and agreement disagreement, there is any loss of substance? Learn, then, from this that substance is not evil; but as in the body, by change of form for the worse, beauty is lost, or rather lessened, and what was called fair before is said to be ugly, and what was pleasing becomes displeasing, so in the mind the seemliness of a right will, which makes a just and pious life, is injured when the will changes for the worse; and by this sin the mind becomes miserable, instead of enjoying as before the happiness which comes from the ornament of a right will, without any gain or loss of substance.

30. Consider, again, that though we admit that the border of the region of darkness was evil for other reasons, such as that it was dim and dark, or any other

reason, still it was not evil in being straight. So, if I admit that there was some evil in its color, you must admit that there was some good in its straightness. Whatever the amount of this good, it is not allowable to attribute it to any other than God the Maker, from whom we must believe that all good in whatsoever nature comes, if we are to escape deadly error. It is absurd, then, to say that this region is perfect evil, when in its straightness of border is found the good of not a little beauty of a material kind; and also to make this region to be altogether estranged, from the almighty and good God, when this good which we find in it can be attributed to no other but the author of all good things. But this border, too, we are told, was evil. Well, suppose it evil: it would surely have been worse had it been crooked instead of straight. And how can that be the perfection of evil than which something worse than itself can be thought of? And to be worse implies that there is some good, the want of which makes the thing worse. Here the want of straightness would make the line worse. Therefore its straightness is something good. And you will never answer the question whence this goodness comes, without reference to Him from whom we must acknowledge that all good things come, whether small or great. But now we shall pass on from considering this border to something else.

Chapter 28. —Manichæus Places Five Natures in the Region of Darkness.

31. "There dwelt," he says, "in that region fiery bodies, destructive races." By speaking of dwelling, he must mean that those bodies were animated and in life.

But, not to appear to cavil at a word, let us see how he divides into five classes all these inhabitants of this region. "Here," he says, "was boundless darkness, flowing from the same source in immeasurable abundance, with the productions properly belonging to it. Beyond this were muddy turbid waters, with their inhabitants; and inside of them winds terrible and violent, with their prince and their progenitors. Then, again, a fiery region of destruction, with its chiefs and peoples. And, similarly, inside of this a race full of smoke and gloom, where abode the dreadful prince and chief of all, having around him innumerable princes, himself the mind and source of them all. Such are the five natures of the pestiferous region." We find here five natures mentioned as part of one nature, which he calls the pestiferous region. The natures are darkness, waters, winds, fire, smoke; which he so arranges as to make darkness first, beginning at the outside. Inside of darkness he puts the waters; inside of the waters, the winds; inside of the winds, the fire; inside of the fire, the smoke. And each of these natures had its peculiar kind of inhabitants, which were likewise five in number. For to the question, Whether there was only one kind in all, or different kinds corresponding to the different natures; the reply is, that they were different: as in other books we find it stated that the darkness had serpents; the waters swimming creatures, such as fish; the winds flying creatures, such as birds; the fire quadrupeds, such as horses, lions, and the like; the smoke bipeds, such as men.

Chapter 29. —The Refutation of This Absurdity.

32. Whose arrangement, then, is this? Who made the distinctions and the classification? Who gave the number, the qualities, the forms, the life? For all these things are in themselves good, nor could each of the natures have them except from the bestowal of God, the author of all good things. For this is not like the descriptions or suppositions of poets about an imaginary chaos, as being a shapeless mass, without form, without quality, without measurement, without weight and number, without order and variety; a confused something, absolutely destitute of qualities, so that some Greek writers call it ἄποιον. So far from being like this is the Manichæan description of the region of darkness, as they call it, that, in a directly contrary style, they add side to side, and join border to border; they number five natures; they separate, arrange, and assign to each its own qualities. Nor do they leave the natures barren or waste, but people them with their proper inhabitants; and to these, again, they give suitable forms, and adapted to their place of habitation, besides giving the chief of all endowments, life. To recount such good things as these, and to speak of them as having no connection with God, the author of all good things, is to lose sight of the excellence of the order in the things, and of the great evil of the error which leads to such a conclusion.

Chapter 30. —The Number of Good Things in Those Natures Which Manichæus Places in the Region of Darkness.

33. "But," is the reply, "the orders of beings inhabiting those five natures were fierce and destructive." As if I were praising their fierceness and destructiveness. I, you see, join with you in condemning the evils you attribute to them; join you with me in praising the good things which you ascribe to them: so it will appear that there is a mixture of good and evil in what you call the last extremity of evil. If I join you in condemning what is mischievous in this region, you must join with me in praising what is beneficial. For these beings could not have been produced, or nourished, or have continued to inhabit that region, without some salutary influence. I join with you in condemning the darkness; join with me in praising the productiveness. For while you call the darkness immeasurable, you speak of "suitable productions." Darkness, indeed, is not a real substance, and means no more than the absence of light, as nakedness means the want of clothing, and emptiness the want of material contents: so that darkness could produce nothing, although a region in darkness—that is, in the absence of light—might produce something. But passing over this for the present, it is certain that where productions arise there must be a beneficent adaptation of substances, as well as a symmetrical arrangement and construction in unity of the members of the beings produced, —a wise adjustment making them agree with one another. And who will deny that all these things are more to be praised than darkness is to be condemned? If I join with you in condemning the muddiness of the waters,

you must join with me in praising the waters as far as they possessed the form and quality of water, and also the agreement of the members of the inhabitants swimming in the waters, their life sustaining and directing their body, and every particular adaptation of substances for the benefit of health. For though you find fault with the waters as turbid and muddy, still, in allowing them the quality of producing and maintaining their living inhabitants, you imply that there was some kind of bodily form, and similarity of parts, giving unity and congruity of character; otherwise there could be no body at all: and, as a rational being, you must see that all these things are to be praised. And however great you make the ferocity of these inhabitants, and their massacrings and devastations in their assaults, you still leave them the regular limits of form, by which the members of each body are made to agree together, and their beneficial adaptations, and the regulating power of the living principle binding together the parts of the body in a friendly and harmonious union. And if all these are regarded with common sense it will be seen that they are more to be commended than the faults are to be condemned. I join with you in condemning the frightfulness of the winds; join with me in praising their nature, as giving breath and nourishment, and their material form in its continuousness and diffusion by the connection of its parts: for by these things these winds had the power of producing and nourishing, and sustaining in vigor these inhabitants you speak of; and also in these inhabitants—besides the other things which have already been commended in all animated creatures—this particular power of going quickly and easily whence and whither they please, and the harmonious stroke of their wings in flight, and their regular motion. I join with you in condemning the destructiveness of fire; join with me in commending the productiveness of this fire, and the growth of these productions, and the adaptation of the fire to the beings produced, so that they had coherence, and came to perfection in measure and shape, and could live and have their abode there: for you see that all these things deserve admiration and praise, not only in the fire which is thus habitable, but in the inhabitants too. I join with you in condemning the denseness of smoke, and the savage character of the prince who, as you say, abode in it; join with me in praising the similarity of all the parts in this very smoke, by which it preserves the harmony and proportion of its parts among themselves, according to its own nature, and has a unity which makes it what it is: for no one can calmly reflect on these things without wonder and praise. Besides, even to the smoke you give the power and energy of production, for you say that princes inhabited it; so that in that region the smoke is productive, which never happens here, and, moreover, affords a wholesome dwelling place to its inhabitants.

Chapter 31. —The Same Subject Continued.

34. And even in the prince of smoke himself, instead of mentioning only his ferocity as a bad quality, ought you not to have taken notice of the other things in his nature which you must allow to be commendable? For he had a soul and a body; the soul life-giving, and the body endowed with life. Since the soul governed and the body obeyed, the soul took the lead and the body followed; the soul gave consistency, the body was not

dissolved; the soul gave harmonious motion, and the body was constructed of a well-proportioned framework of members. In this single prince are you not induced to express approval of the orderly peace or the peaceful order? And what applies to one applies to all the rest. You say he was fierce and cruel to others. This is not what I commend, but the other important things which you will not take notice of. Those things, when perceived and considered, —after advice by anyone who has without consideration put faith in Manichæus, —lead him to a clear conviction that, in speaking of those natures, he speaks of things good in a sense, not perfect and uncreated, like God the one Trinity, nor of the higher rank of created things, like the holy angels and the ever-blessed powers; but of the lowest class, and ranked according to the small measure of their endowments. These things are thought to be blameworthy by the uninstructed when they compare them with higher things; and in view of their want of some good, the good they have gets the name of evil, because it is defective. My reason also for thus discussing the natures enumerated by Manichæus is that the things named are things familiar to us in this world. We are familiar with darkness, waters, winds, fire, smoke; we are familiar, too, with animals, creeping, swimming, flying; with quadrupeds and biped. With the exception of darkness (which, as I have said already, is nothing but the absence of light, and the perception of it is only the absence of sight, as the perception of silence is the absence of hearing; not that darkness is anything, but that light is not, as neither that silence is anything, but that sound is not), all the other things are natural qualities and are familiar to all; and the form of those natures, which is commendable and good as far as it exists, no wise man attributes to any other author than God, the author of all good things.

Chapter 32. —Manichæus Got the Arrangement of His Fanciful Notions from Visible Objects.

35. For in giving to these natures which he has learned from visible things, an arrangement according to his fanciful ideas, to represent the race of darkness, Manichæus is clearly in error. First of all, he makes darkness productive, which is impossible. But, he replies, this darkness was unlike what you are familiar with. How, then, can you make me understand about it? After so many promises to give knowledge, will you force me to take your word for it? Suppose I believe you, this at least is certain, that if the darkness had no form, as darkness usually has not, it could produce nothing; if it had form, it was better than ordinary darkness: whereas, when you call it different from the ordinary kind, you wish us to believe that it is worse. You might as well say that silence, which is the same to the ear as darkness to the eyes, produced some deaf or dumb animals in that region; and then, in reply to the objection that silence is not a nature, you might say that it was different silence from ordinary silence; in a word, you might say what you pleased to those whom you have once misled into believing you. No doubt, the obvious facts relating to the origin of animal life led Manichæus to say that serpents were produced in darkness. However, there are serpents which have such sharp sight, and such pleasure in light, that they seem to give evidence of the most weighty kind against this idea. Then the idea of swimming things in the water might easily be got here, and applied to the fanciful

objects in that region; and so of flying things in the winds, for the motion of the lower air in this world, where birds fly, is called wind. Where he got the idea of the quadrupeds in fire, no one can tell. Still he said this deliberately, though without sufficient thought, and from great misconception. The reason usually given is, that quadrupeds are voracious and salacious. But many men surpass any quadruped in voracity, though they are bipeds, and are called children of the smoke, and not of fire. Geese, too, are as voracious as any animal; and though he might place them in fire as bipeds, or in the water because they love to swim, or in the winds because they have wings and sometimes fly, they certainly have nothing to do with fire in this classification. About salaciousness, I suppose he was thinking of neighing horses, which sometimes bite through the bridle and rush at the mares; and writing hastily, with this in his mind, he forgot the common sparrow, in comparison of which the hottest stallion is cold. The reason they give for assigning bipeds to the smoke is, that bipeds are conceited and proud, for men are derived from this class; and the idea, which is a plausible one, is that smoke resembles proud people in rising up into the air, round and swelling. This idea might warrant a figurative description of proud men, or an allegorical expression or explanation, but not the belief that bipeds are born in smoke and of smoke. They might with equal reason be said to be born in dust, for it often rises up to the heaven with a similar circling and lofty motion; or in the clouds, for they are often drawn up from the earth in such a way, that those looking from a distance are uncertain whether they are clouds or smoke. Once more, why, in the case of the waters and the winds, does he suit the inhabitants to the character of the place, as we see swimming things in water, and flying things in the wind; whereas, in the face of fire and smoke, this bold liar is not ashamed to assign to these places the most unlikely inhabitants? For fire burns quadrupeds, and consumes them, and smoke suffocates and kills bipeds. At least he must acknowledge that he has made these natures better in the race of darkness than they are here, though he wishes us to think everything to be worse. For, according to this, the fire there produced and nourished quadrupeds, and gave them a lodging not only harmless, but most convenient. The smoke, too, provided room for the offspring of its own benign bosom, and cherished them up to the rank of prince. Thus we see that these lies, which have added to the number of heretics, arose from the perception by carnal sense, only without care or discernment, of visible objects in this world, and when thus conceived, were brought forth by fancy, and then presumptuously written and published.

Chapter 33. —Every Nature, as Nature, is Good.

36. But the consideration we wish most to urge is the truth of the Catholic doctrine, if they can understand it, that God is the author of all natures. I urged this before when I said, I join with you in your condemnation of destructiveness, of blindness, of dense muddiness, of terrific violence, of perishableness, of the ferocity of the princes, and so on; join with me in commending form, classification, arrangement, harmony, unity of structure, symmetry and correspondence of members, provision for vital breath and nourishment, wholesome adaptation, regulation and control by the mind, and the subjection of the bodies, and the assimilation and agreement of parts in

the natures, both those inhabiting and those inhabited, and all the other things of the same kind. From this, if they would only think honestly, they would understand that it implies a mixture of good and evil, even in the region where they suppose evil to be alone and in perfection: so that if the evils mentioned were taken away, the good things will remain, without anything to detract from the commendation given to them; whereas, if the good things are taken away, no nature is left. From this everyone sees, who can see, that every nature, as far as it is nature, is good; since in one and the same thing in which I found something to praise, and he found something to blame, if the good things are taken away, no nature will remain; but if the disagreeable things are taken away, the nature will remain unimpaired. Take from waters their thickness and muddiness, and pure clear water remains; take from them the consistence of their parts, and no water will be left. If then, after the evil is removed, the nature remains in a purer state, and does not remain at all when the good is taken away, it must be the good which makes the nature of the thing in which it is, while the evil is not nature, but contrary to nature. Take from the winds their terribleness and excessive force, with which you find fault, you can conceive of winds as gentle and mild; take from them the similarity of their parts which gives them continuity of substance, and the unity essential to material existence, and no nature remains to be conceived of. It would be tedious to go through all the cases; but all who consider the subject free from party spirit must see that in their list of natures the disagreeable things mentioned are additions to the nature; and when they are removed, the natures remain better than before. This shows that the natures, as far as they are natures, are good; for when you take from them the good instead of the evil, no natures remain. And attend, you who wish to arrive at a correct judgment, to what is said of the fierce prince himself. If you take away his ferocity, see how many excellent things will remain; his material frame, the symmetry of the members on one side with those on the other, the unity of his form, the settled continuity of his parts, the orderly adjustment of the mind as ruling and animating, and the body as subject and animated. The removal of these things, and of others I may have omitted to mention, will leave no nature remaining.

Chapter 34. —Nature Cannot Be Without Some Good. The Manichæans Dwell Upon the Evils.

37. But perhaps you will say that these evils cannot be removed from the natures, and must therefore be considered natural. The question at present is not what can be taken away, and what cannot; but it certainly helps to a clear perception that these natures, as far as they are natures, are good, when we see that the good things can be thought of without these evil things, while without these good things no nature can be conceived of. I can conceive of waters without muddy commotion; but without settled continuity of parts no material form is an object of thought or of sensation in any way. Therefore, even these muddy waters could not exist without the good which was the condition of their material existence. As to the reply that these evil things cannot be taken from such natures, I rejoin that neither can the good things be taken away. Why, then, should you call these things natural evils, on account of the evil things which you suppose cannot be taken away, and yet refuse to call them natural

good things, on account of the good things which, as has been proved, cannot be taken away?

38. You may next ask, as you usually do for a last resource, whence come these evils which I have said that I too disapprove of. I shall perhaps tell you, if you first tell me whence are those good things which you too are obliged to commend, if you would not be altogether unreasonable. But why should I ask this, when we both acknowledge that all good things whatever, and how great soever, are from the one God, who is supremely good? You must therefore yourselves oppose Manichæus who has placed all these important good things which we have mentioned and justly commended, —the continuity and agreement of parts in each nature, the health and vigor of the animated creatures, and the other things which it would be wearisome to repeat, — (in an imaginary region of darkness, so as to separate them altogether from that God whom he allows to be the author of all good things.) He lost sight of those good things, while taking notice only of what was disagreeable; as if one, frightened by a lion's roaring, and seeing him dragging away and tearing the bodies of cattle or human beings which he had seized, should from childish pusillanimity be so overpowered with fear as to see nothing but the cruelty and ferocity of the lion; and overlooking or disregarding all the other qualities, should exclaim against the nature of this animal as not only evil, but a great evil, his fear adding to his vehemence. But were he to see a tame lion, with its ferocity subdued, especially if he had never been frightened by a lion, he would have leisure, in the absence of danger and terror, to observe and admire the beauty of the animal. My only remark on this is one closely connected with our subject: that any nature may be in

some case disagreeable, so as to excite hatred towards the whole nature; though it is clear that the form of a real living beast, even when it excites terror in the woods, is far better than that of the artificial imitation which is commended in a painting on the wall. We must not then be misled into this error by Manichæus, or be hindered from observing the forms of the natures, by his finding fault with some things in them in such a way as to make us disapprove of them entirely, when it is impossible to show that they deserve entire disapproval. And when our minds are thus composed and prepared to form a just judgment, we may ask whence come those evils which I have said that I condemn. It will be easier to see this if we class them all under one name.

Chapter 35. —Evil Alone is Corruption. Corruption is Not Nature, But Contrary to Nature. Corruption Implies Previous Good.

39. For who can doubt that the whole of that which is called evil is nothing else than corruption? Different evils may, indeed, be called by different names; but that which is the evil of all things in which any evil is perceptible is corruption. So the corruption of an educated mind is ignorance; the corruption of a prudent mind is imprudence; the corruption of a just mind, injustice; the corruption of a brave mind, cowardice; the corruption of a calm, peaceful mind, cupidity, fear, sorrow, pride. Again, in a living body, the corruption of health is pain and disease; the corruption of strength is exhaustion; the corruption of rest is toil. Again, in any corporeal thing, the corruption of beauty is ugliness; the corruption of straightness is crookedness; the corruption

of order is confusion; the corruption of entireness is disseverance, or fracture, or diminution. It would be long and laborious to mention by name all the corruptions of the things here mentioned, and of countless other things; for in many cases the words may apply to the mind as well as to the body, and in innumerable cases the corruption has a distinct name of its own. But enough has been said to show that corruption does harm only as displacing the natural condition; and so, that corruption is not nature, but against nature. And if corruption is the only evil to be found anywhere, and if corruption is not nature, no nature is evil.

40. But if, perchance, you cannot follow this, consider again, that whatever is corrupted is deprived of some good: for if it were not corrupted, it would be incorrupt; or if it could not in any way be corrupted, it would be incorruptible. Now, if corruption is an evil, both incorruption and incorruptibility must be good things. We are not, however, speaking at present of incorruptible nature, but of things which admit of corruption, and which, while not corrupted, may be called incorrupt, but not incorruptible. That alone can be called incorruptible which not only is not corrupted, but also cannot in any part be corrupted. Whatever things, then, being incorrupt, but liable to corruption, begin to be corrupted, are deprived of the good which they had as incorrupt. Nor is this a slight good, for corruption is a great evil. And the continued increase of corruption implies the continued presence of good, of which they may be deprived. Accordingly, the natures supposed to exist in the region of darkness must have been either corruptible or incorruptible. If they were incorruptible, they were in possession of a good than which nothing is

higher. If they were corruptible, they were either corrupted or not corrupted. If they were not corrupted, they were incorrupt, to say which of anything is to give it great praise. If they were corrupted, they were deprived of this great good of incorruption; but the deprivation implies the previous possession of the good they are deprived of; and if they possessed this good, they were not the perfection of evil, and consequently all the Manichæan story is a falsehood.

Chapter 36. —The Source of Evil or of Corruption of Good.

41. After thus inquiring what evil is, and learning that it is not nature, but against nature, we must next inquire whence it is. If Manichæus had done this, he might have escaped falling into the snare of these serious errors. Out of time and out of order, he began with inquiring into the origin of evil, without first asking what evil was; and so his inquiry led him only to the reception of foolish fancies, of which the mind, much fed by the bodily senses, with difficulty rids itself. Perhaps, then, someone, desiring no longer argument, but delivery from error, will ask, Whence is this corruption which we find to be the common evil of good things which are not incorruptible? Such an inquirer will soon find the answer if he seeks for truth with great earnestness, and knocks reverently with sustained assiduity. For while man can use words as a kind of sign for the expression of his thoughts, teaching is the work of the incorruptible Truth itself, who is the one true, the one internal Teacher. He became external also, that He might recall us from the external to the internal; and taking on Himself the form of

a servant, that He might bring down His height to the knowledge of those rising up to Him, He condescended to appear in lowliness to the low. In His name let us ask, and through Him let us seek mercy of the Father while making this inquiry. For to answer in a word the question, Whence is corruption? it is hence, because these natures that are capable of corruption were not begotten by God, but made by Him out of nothing; and as we already proved that those natures are good, no one can say with propriety that they were not good as made by God. If it is said that God made them perfectly good, it must be remembered that the only perfect good is God Himself, the maker of those good things.

Chapter 37. —God Alone Perfectly Good.

42. What harm, you ask, would follow if those things too were perfectly good? Still, should anyone, who admits and believes the perfect goodness of God the Father, inquire what source we should reverently assign to any other perfectly good thing, supposing it to exist, our only correct reply would be, that it is of God the Father, who is perfectly good. And we must bear in mind that what is of Him is born of Him, and not made by Him out of nothing, and that it is therefore perfectly, that is, incorruptibly, good like God Himself. So we see that it is unreasonable to require that things made out of nothing should be as perfectly good as He who was begotten of God Himself, and who is one as God is one, otherwise God would have begotten something unlike Himself. Hence it shows ignorance and impiety to seek for brethren for this only-begotten Son through whom all good things were made by the Father out of nothing, except in this,

that He condescended to appear as man. Accordingly in Scripture He is called both only-begotten and first-begotten; only-begotten of the Father, and first-begotten from the dead. "And we beheld," says John, "His glory, the glory as of the only-begotten of the Father, full of grace and truth." And Paul says, "that He might be the first-born among many brethren."

43. But should we say, These things made out of nothing are not good things, but only God's nature is good, we shall be unjust to good things of great value. And there is impiety in calling it a defect in anything not to be what God is, and in denying a thing to be good because it is inferior to God. Pray submit then, thou nature of the rational soul, to be somewhat less than God, but only so far less, that after Him nothing else is above thee. Submit, I say, and yield to Him, lest He drive thee still lower into depths where the punishment inflicted will continually detract more and more from the good which thou hast. Thou exalts thyself against God, if thou art indignant at His preceding thee; and thou art very contumacious in thy thoughts of Him, if thou dost not rejoice unspeakably in the possession of this good, that He alone is above thee. This being settled as certain, thou art not to say, God should have made me the only nature: there should be no good thing after me. It could not be that the next good thing to God should be the last. And in this is seen most clearly how great dignity God conferred on thee, that He who in the order of nature alone rules over thee, made other good things for thee to rule over. Nor be surprised that they are not now in all respects subject to thee, and that sometimes they pain thee; for thy Lord has greater authority over the things subject to thee than thou hast, as a master over the servants of his

servants. What wonder, then, if, when thou sins, that is, disobeys thy Lord, the things thou before rules over are made instrumental in thy punishment? For what is so just, or what is more just than God? For this befell human nature in Adam, of whom this is not the place to speak. Suffice it to say, the righteous Ruler acts in character both in just rewards and in just punishments, in the happiness of those who live rightly, and in the penalty inflicted on sinners. Nor yet art thou left without mercy, since by an appointed distribution of things and times thou art called to return. Thus the righteous control of the supreme Creator extends even to earthly good things, which are corrupted and restored, that thou might have consolations mingled with punishments; that thou might both praise God when delighted by the order of good things, and might take refuge in Him when tried by experience of evils. So, as far as earthly things are subject to thee, they teach thee that thou art their ruler; as far as they distress thee, they teach thee to be subject to thy Lord.

Chapter 38. —Nature Made by God; Corruption Comes from Nothing.

44. In this way, though corruption is an evil, and though it comes not from the Author of natures, but from their being made out of nothing, still, in God's government and control over all that He has made, even corruption is so ordered that it hurts only the lowest natures, for the punishment of the condemned, and for the trial and instruction of the returning, that they may keep near to the incorruptible God, and remain incorrupt, which is our only good; as is said by the prophet, "But it is good for me that I keep near to God." And you must

not say, God did not make corruptible natures: for, as far as they are natures, God made them; but as far as they are corruptible, God did not make them: for corruption cannot come from Him who alone is incorruptible. If you can receive this, give thanks to God; if you cannot, be quiet and do not condemn what you do not yet understand, but humbly wait on Him who is the light of the mind that thou mayest know. For in the expression "corruptible nature" there are two words, and not one only. So, in the expression, God made out of nothing, "God" and "nothing" are two separate words. Render therefore to each of these words that which belongs to each, so that the word "nature" may go with the word "God," "and the word "corruptible" with the word "nothing." And yet even the corruptions, though they have not their origin from God, are to be overruled by Him in accordance with the order of inanimate things and the deserts of His intelligent creatures. Thus, we say rightly that reward and punishment are both from God. For God's not making corruption is consistent with His giving over to corruption the man who deserves to be corrupted, that is, who has begun to corrupt himself by sinning, that he who has willfully yielded to the allurements of corruption may, against his will, suffer its pains.

Chapter 39. —In What Sense Evils are from God.

45. Not only is it written in the Old Testament, "I make good, and create evil;" but more clearly in the New Testament, where the Lord says, "Fear not them which kill the body, and have no more that they can do; but fear him who, after he has killed the body, has power to cast

the soul into hell." And that to voluntary corruption penal corruption is added in the divine judgment, is plainly declared by the Apostle Paul, when he says, "The temple of God is holy, which temple ye are; whoever corrupts the temple of God, him will God corrupt." If this had been said in the Old Law, how vehemently would the Manichæans have denounced it as making God a corrupter! And from fear of the word, many Latin translators make it, "him shall God destroy," instead of corrupt, avoiding the offensive word without any change of meaning. Although these would inveigh against any passage in the Old Law or the prophets if God was called in it a destroyer. But the Greek original here shows that corrupt is the true word; for it is written distinctly, "Whoever corrupts the temple of God, him will God corrupt." If the Manichæans are asked to explain the words, they will say, to escape making God a corrupter, that corrupt here means to give over to corruption, or some such explanation. Did they read the Old Law in this spirit, they would both find many admirable things in it; and instead of spitefully attacking passages which they did not understand, they would reverently postpone the inquiry.

Chapter 40. —Corruption Tends to Non-Existence.

46. But if any one does not believe that corruption comes from nothing, let him place before himself existence and non-existence—one, as it were, on one side, and the other on the other (to speak so as not to outstrip the slow to understand); then let him set something, say the body of an animal, between them, and let him ask

himself whether, while the body is being formed and produced, while its size is increasing, while it gains nourishment, health, strength, beauty, stability, it is tending, as regards its duration and permanence, to this side or that, to existence or non-existence. He will see without difficulty, that even in the rudimentary form there is an existence, and that the more the body is established and built up in form, and figure and strength, the more does it come to exist, and to tend to the side of existence. Then, again, let the body begin to be corrupted; let its whole condition be enfeebled, let its vigor languish, its strength decay, its beauty be defaced, its framework be sundered, the consistency of its parts give way and go to pieces; and let him ask now where the body is tending in this corruption, whether to existence or non-existence: he will not surely be so blind or stupid as to doubt how to answer himself, or as not to see that, in proportion as anything is corrupted, in that proportion it approaches decease. But whatever tends to decease tends to non-existence. Since, then, we must believe that God exists immutably and incorruptibly, while what is called nothing is clearly altogether nonexistent; and since, after setting before yourself existence and non-existence, you have observed that the more a visible object increases the more it tends towards existence, while the more it is corrupted the more it tends towards non-existence, why are you at a loss to tell regarding any nature what in it is from God, and what from nothing; seeing that visible form is natural, and corruption against nature? The increase of form leads to existence, and we acknowledge God as supreme existence; the increase of corruption leads to non-existence, and we know that what is non-existent is nothing. Why then, I say, are you at a loss to tell regarding a corruptible nature, when you have both the words nature and corruptible, what is from God, and what from nothing? And why do you inquire for a nature contrary to God, since, if you confess that He is the supreme existence, it follows that non-existence is contrary to Him?

Chapter 41. —Corruption is by God's Permission, and Comes from Us.

47. You ask, Why does corruption take from nature what God has given to it? It takes nothing but where God permits; and He permits in righteous and well-ordered judgment, according to the degrees of non-intelligent and the deserts of intelligent creatures. The word uttered passes away as an object of sense, and perishes in silence; and yet the coming and going of these passing words make our speech, and the regular intervals of silence give pleasing and appropriate distinction; and so it is with temporal natures which have this lowest form of beauty, that transition gives them being, and the death of what they give birth to gives them individuality. And if our sense and memory could rightly take in the order and proportions of this beauty, it would so please us, that we should not dare to give the name of corruptions to those imperfections which give rise to the distinction. And when distress comes to us through their peculiar beauty, by the loss of beloved temporal things passing away, we both pay the penalty of our sins, and are exhorted to set our affection on eternal things.

Chapter 42. —Exhortation to the Chief Good.

48. Let us, then, not seek in this beauty for what has not been given to it (and from not having what we seek for, this is the lowest form of beauty); and in that which has been given to it, let us praise God, because He has bestowed this great good of visible form even on the lowest degree of beauty. And let us not cleave as lovers to this beauty, but as praisers of God let us rise above it; and from this superior position let us pronounce judgment on it, instead of so being bound up in it as to be judged along with it. And let us hasten on to that good which has no motion in space or advancement in time, from which all natures in space and time receive their sensible being and their form. To see this good let us purify our heart by faith in our Lord Jesus Christ, who says, "Blessed are the pure in heart, for they shall see God." For the eyes needed in order to see this good are not those with which we see the light spread through space, which has part in one place and part in another, instead of being all in every place. The sight and the discernment we are to purify is that by which we see, as far as is allowed in this life, what is just, what is pious, what is the beauty of wisdom. He who sees these things, values them far above the fullness of all regions in space, and finds that the vision of these things requires not the extension of his perception through distances in space, but its invigoration by an immaterial influence.

Chapter 43. —Conclusion.

49. And as this vision is greatly hindered by those fancies which are originated by the carnal sense, and are retained and modified by the imagination, let us abhor this heresy which has been led by faith in its fancies to represent the divine substance as extended and diffused through space, even through infinite space, and to cut short one side so as to make room for evil,—not being able to perceive that evil is not nature, but against nature; and to beautify this very evil with such visible appearance, and forms, and consistency of parts prevailing in its several natures, not being able to conceive of any nature without those good things, that the evils found fault with in it are buried under a countless abundance of good things.

Here let us close this part of the treatise. The other absurdities of Manichæus will be exposed in what follows, by the permission and help of God.

www.ingramcontent.com/pod-product-compliance
Lightning Source LLC
Chambersburg PA
CBHW052117070526
44584CB00017B/2521